TOUGH TRUCKS

D1224452

To Billy, Arthur, Sophie, Guy and Jan – T.M.
For Frank – A.P.

The Publisher thanks the Road Haulage Association in the UK, the Chicago Department of Streets and Sanitation, and the National Truck Equipment Association in the US for their kind assistance in the development of this book.

KINGFISHER

First published by Kingfisher 2003
This edition published by Kingfisher 2007
an imprint of Macmillan Children's Books
a division of Macmillan Publishers Limited
20 New Wharf Road, London N1 9RR
Basingstoke and Oxford
Associated companies throughout the world
www.panmacmillan.com

ISBN: 978-0-7534-1522-1

Text copyright © Tony Mitton 2003 Illustrations copyright © Ant Parker 2003
The moral right of the author and illustrator has been asserted.

All rights reserved. No part of this publication may be reproduced, stored in or introduced into a retrieval system, or transmitted, in any form or by any means (electronic, mechanical, photocopying, recording or otherwise), without the prior written permission of the publisher. Any person who does any unauthorized act in relation to this publication may be liable to criminal prosecution and civil claims for damages.

3 5 7 9 10 8 6 4 2

A CIP catalogue record for this book is available from the British Library.

Printed in China

This book is sold subject to the condition that it shall not, by way of trade or otherwise, be lent, resold, hired out, or otherwise circulated without the publisher's prior consent in any form of binding or cover other than that in which it is published and without a similar condition including this condition being imposed on the subsequent purchaser.

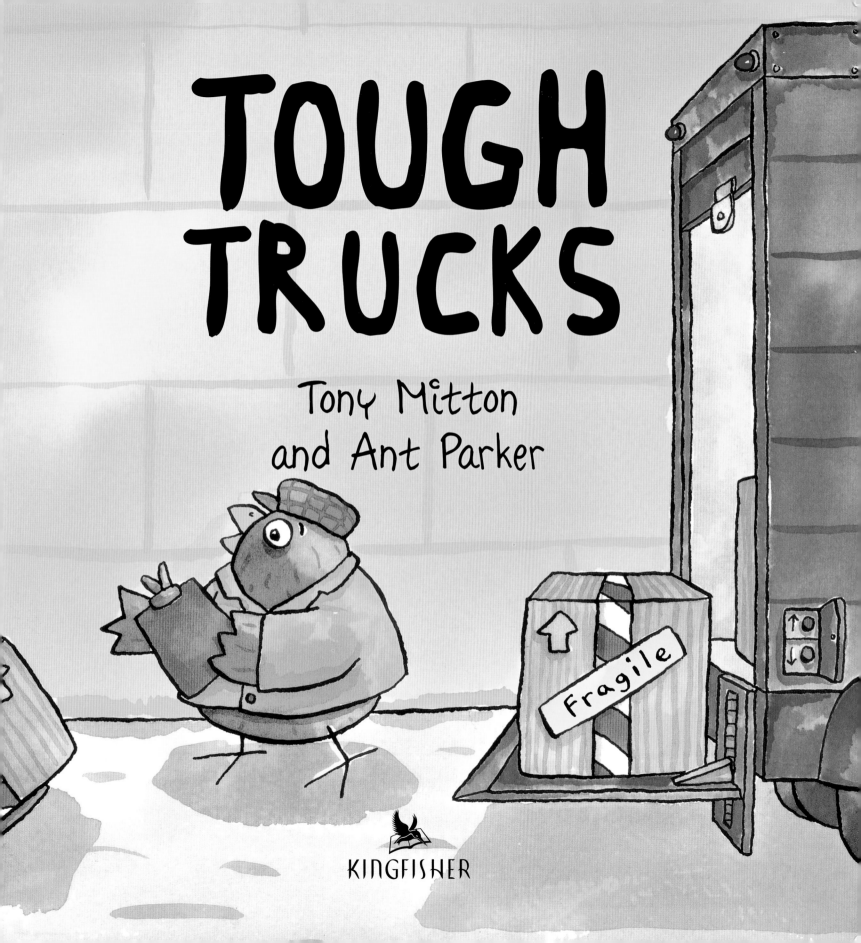

TOUGH TRUCKS

Tony Mitton
and Ant Parker

KINGFISHER

rumble

Trucks are tough and sturdy.
They take on heavy loads,

rumble

**then thunder on their giant tyres
down long and busy roads.**

A truck has got a cab up front.
The driver sits inside.
The truck's controls are all around,
ready for the ride.

The driver starts the engine
and, when the way is clear,
accelerates along the road
and turns the wheel to steer.

Some truck cabs have a bunk bed,
a curtain and a light

to make a tiny bedroom
where the driver sleeps at night.

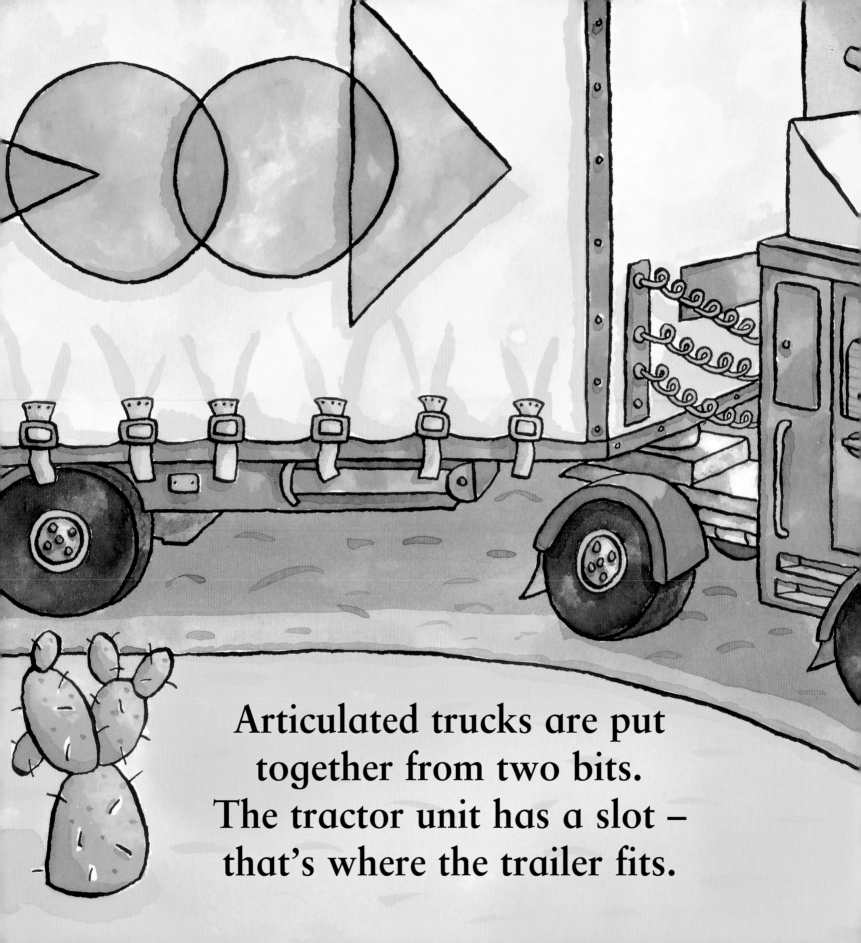

Articulated trucks are put
together from two bits.
The tractor unit has a slot –
that's where the trailer fits.

So when the truck is travelling
on roads that weave and wend,
the separate bits turn one by one
to get around a bend.

A refuse truck collects the rubbish,
grumbling down the street.

It lifts the bins and empties them
to keep things clean and neat.

A concrete mixer stirs its load
while travelling to the site.
The foreman points, "Just pour it here.
We're ready now. Alright?"

The piston on a tipper truck
can push to tilt it up.
We're just about to dump some rubble.
Ready, steady, hup!

A tanker carries liquids,
so it's sealed up good and tight.

This shiny tanker's full of milk,
all creamy, cool and white.

When travelling long distances,
you're on the road alone,
so drivers keep in touch
by CB radio, or phone.

This truck has had a breakdown,
but the driver didn't panic.
He radioed around and found
a handy truck mechanic.

Driving trucks is tiring,
but you need to be awake.

So drivers call at truck stops
for a meal or a break.

But look, we've reached the depot.
We've made another run.

The forklift starts unloading,
and the foreman shouts, "Well done!"

Truck bits

articulated truck

sometimes called an **artic**, this is made up of a tractor and a trailer

cab

this is where the driver si‘

trailer

this holds the truck's load

tractor

this pulls the trailer

CB radio

a driver can use this special radio to talk to other drivers

piston

also called a **ram**, this is a strong pump that pushes up the back of a tipper truck to dump its load